INTRODUCTION TO COMPOSITION

Student Guide

Brenda Janke & Jessica Watson

MEMORIA PRESS

MEMORIA PRESS
www.MemoriaPress.com

INTRODUCTION TO COMPOSITION

STUDENT GUIDE
Brenda Janke & Jessica Watson

ISBN 978-1-61538-849-3

Cover illustration by Henriette Browne, late 1800s

Contents

How to Teach Composition

The goal of composition in third grade is to teach correct and expressive writing to the students through modeling. This can be done effectively by formulating and editing sentences together as a class, with the teacher functioning as the primary editor.

GUIDED LESSON:

Complete one lesson in the workbook per week.
The dictation sentences at the end of the lessons are loosely coordinated with the progression of grammar rules taught in the third grade grammar book.
As the year progresses, students may be given more freedom to write or edit some parts on their own, however, modeling should remain the primary lesson format.

Reading Passage:

Read the selection referenced. This is best done with the teacher reading orally and the students following along in their own books.

Guided Questions:

Read the questions together orally BEFORE reading the passage in the book. Answers are not meant to be written out, but should rather be used to guide students to the three main points in the following outline section.

Outline:

Using each guided question in turn, discuss and formulate a short sentence together as a class to summarize the answer. Do not focus on elevated language or perfect editing at this point. A simple statement to answer the question is best.

Summary:

A. Using the simple outline sentences, work together as a class to formulate three well-written summary sentences.

B. Allow several individual students to offer suggestions. After hearing a few sentences, ask students to think of the given responses, pulling together the best parts of each one.

C. Then begin again, asking for a good summary sentence, this time writing their exact words on the board. If adequate sentences are not forthcoming, the teacher may offer the example in the Teacher Key (or a similar form of it) to discuss together. It is not necessary to end up with the exact sentence in the Teacher Key, which is merely offered as an example.

D. Work sentence by sentence, following the outline closely, writing each sentence on the board. The students are not writing anything in their books at this point. This is meant to be a focused discussion and modeling time.

E. Using the following guidelines, edit your summary together. Students are still just listening and contributing to the work on the board, not writing.
   1. Use all verbs in the same tense.
   2. Look for repeated words, and consider replacing them with synonyms.
   3. Use pronouns instead of repeating the same name multiple times.
   4. Replace insipid verbs and adjectives with vivid, descriptive ones.
   5. Check capitalization, punctuation, and spelling.

F. When editing is complete, rewrite the three-sentence summary on the board in perfect form for the students to copy.

G. Read the summary aloud together as a class, enjoying the final result their hard work has produced.

H. Students copy the summary, exactly as written, into the summary section of their Student Guides.

Dictation:

A. The teacher reads the sentence from the Dictation section at the end of the lesson three times, aloud, in succession. The students repeat the sentence aloud. They then begin to write it from memory in their Student Guides.*

B. When all students are finished writing, the teacher should indicate any capitalization or unusual punctuation marks that have not yet been covered in the grammar lessons. Students are then allowed to make corrections to their sentences.

C. The teacher then writes the correct sentence on the board. Students check their work against the sentence on the board, making corrections to their own sentence with a red pen.

D. On the following day, the teacher repeats step A, but students should write the sentence on a separate sheet of paper to be turned in for a grade.

*Students who complete the dictation perfectly the first time without help or correction may show their work to the teacher for a grade and may skip the second dictation exercise the following day.

Note: Offer encouragement at all levels of accuracy. This is a learning process. Do not expect perfection in the beginning attempts. The goal is to become more proficient in listening skills and using the grammar rules correctly.

Reading Passage

Read *Farmer Boy*, pp. 11-12, "The sun was shining … Mr. Corse did not say anything."

Guided Questions

1. What happens when the boys go out to play during recess?
2. What do they do when they realize this?
3. How does Mr. Corse respond?

Outline

I. ____

II. ____

III. ____

Student Summary

In three sentences, summarize the passage. Say the sentences out loud to yourself. Then write them below.

Dictation

Reading Passage

Read *Farmer Boy*, pp. 43-45, "Mr. Corse lifted the lid … and slammed and locked the door."

Guided Questions

1. What is Big Bill Ritchie planning to do to the teacher?
2. How does Mr. Corse surprise the class?
3. What finally happens to Big Bill Ritchie?

Outline

I. ______________________________

II. ______________________________

III. ______________________________

Student Summary

In three sentences, summarize the passage. Say the sentences out loud to yourself. Then write them below.

Dictation

Reading Passage

Read *Farmer Boy*, pp. 69-70, "Side by side … did not go near it again."

Guided Questions

1. What happens to Almanzo?
2. Who saves him?
3. How does Almanzo feel, and what does he do differently from then on?

Outline

I. ______________________________

II. ______________________________

III. ______________________________

Student Summary

In three sentences, summarize the passage. Say the sentences out loud to yourself. Then write them below.

____

____

____

____

____

____

____

____

____

Dictation

____

____

____

____

Reading Passage

Read *Farmer Boy*, pp. 98-101, "As soon as the whip was ready … a good yoke of oxen, yet."

Guided Questions

1. How does Almanzo feel while training his oxen?
2. What does he remember about training animals?
3. What is the result of Almanzo's patience?

Outline

I. ______________________________

II. ______________________________

III. ______________________________

Student Summary

In three sentences, summarize the passage. Say the sentences out loud to yourself. Then write them below.

Dictation

Reading Passage

Read *Farmer Boy*, pp. 151-153, "The moon was shining … find his way home again."

Guided Questions

1. What is outside the Wilders' door?
2. What do they learn the following day?
3. What do they believe was the reason the dog came to them?

Outline

I. ____

II. ____

III. ____

Student Summary

In three sentences, summarize the passage. Say the sentences out loud to yourself. Then write them below.

Dictation

Reading Passage

Read *Farmer Boy*, pp. 169-172, "All the corn was … the corn was saved."

Guided Questions

1. How is the corn crop threatened?
2. What do the Wilders do to save the corn?
3. How much of the crop are they able to save?

Outline

I. ____

II. ____

III. ____

Student Summary

In three sentences, summarize the passage. Say the sentences out loud to yourself. Then write them below.

Dictation

Reading Passage

Read *Farmer Boy*, pp. 219-222, "Now, Almanzo, you polish … on the white-and-gold wall."

Guided Questions

1. Why is Almanzo angry, and what does he do?
2. What happens to the parlor wall?
3. How does Almanzo respond?

Outline

I. ______________________________

II. ______________________________

III. ______________________________

Student Summary

In three sentences, summarize the passage. Say the sentences out loud to yourself. Then write them below.

Dictation

Reading Passage

Read *Farmer Boy*, pp. 237-239, "One day when Almanzo … and wonder who made it."

Guided Questions

1. Who comes to the Wilders' farm, and why?
2. How does he show his admiration for Mother's butter?
3. What does Mother do with the money she receives?

Outline

I. ____________________

II. ____________________

III. ____________________

Student Summary

In three sentences, summarize the passage. Say the sentences out loud to yourself. Then write them below.

Dictation

Reading Passage

Read *Farmer Boy*, pp. 296-297, "Eliza Jane was more bossy … shut up Eliza Jane."

Guided Questions

1. Why is Eliza Jane upset?
2. What does Mother have to say about it?
3. How does Eliza Jane respond?

Outline

I. ______________________________

II. ______________________________

III. ______________________________

Student Summary

In three sentences, summarize the passage. Say the sentences out loud to yourself. Then write them below.

____

____

____

____

____

____

____

____

____

____

Dictation

____

____

____

Reading Passage

Read *Farmer Boy*, pp. 315-317, "It was still dark … Father chuckled."

Guided Questions

1. Why is this a special morning?
2. What gifts does Almanzo receive?
3. What do they discover about the time?

Outline

I. ______________________________

II. ______________________________

III. ______________________________

Student Summary

In three sentences, summarize the passage. Say the sentences out loud to yourself. Then write them below.

____

____

____

____

____

____

____

____

____

____

Dictation

____

____

____

Reading Passage

Read *Farmer Boy*, pp. 369-371, "'Father was looking solemn. … I'll give you Starlight."

Guided Questions

1. What decision needs to be made?
2. How does Father try to help Almanzo make this decision?
3. What does Almanzo decide?

Outline

I. ____

II. ____

III. ____

Student Summary

In three sentences, summarize the passage. Say the sentences out loud to yourself. Then write them below.

Dictation

Reading Passage

Read *The Best Christmas Pageant Ever*, pp. 21-23, "But then she got stuck … got stuck with that."

Guided Questions

1. Who is Mrs. Armstrong?
2. What happens to her?
3. How does this affect Mother?

Outline

I. ______________________________

II. ______________________________

III. ______________________________

Student Summary

In three sentences, summarize the passage. Say the sentences out loud to yourself. Then write them below.

____

____

____

____

____

____

____

____

____

____

Dictation

____

____

____

Reading Passage

Read *The Best Christmas Pageant Ever*, pp. 55-57, "Since none of the Herdmans … No Jesus … ever."

Guided Questions

1. What is unusual about the Herdman children?
2. How does this affect the way they act out their parts in the pageant?
3. How does this affect the thinking of the narrator of the story?

Outline

I. ______________________________

II. ______________________________

III. ______________________________

Student Summary

In three sentences, summarize the passage. Say the sentences out loud to yourself. Then write them below.

Dictation

Reading Passage

Read *Charlotte's Web*, pp. 4-7, "Fern came slowly … she whispered to herself."

Guided Questions

1. What does Mr. Arable do during breakfast?
2. How does Fern respond to this gift?
3. What does she name her pet?

Outline

I. ______________________________

II. ______________________________

III. ______________________________

Student Summary

In three sentences, summarize the passage. Say the sentences out loud to yourself. Then write them below.

____

____

____

____

____

____

____

____

____

____

Dictation

____

____

____

Reading Passage

Read *Charlotte's Web*, pp. 39-40, "You mean you eat … a good thing after all."

Guided Questions

1. What unpleasant information does Wilbur learn, and how does he feel about it?
2. What does Charlotte say in response?
3. How does Wilbur change his mind about spiders?

Outline

I. ______________________________

II. ______________________________

III. ______________________________

Student Summary

In three sentences, summarize the passage. Say the sentences out loud to yourself. Then write them below.

Dictation

Reading Passage

Read *Charlotte's Web*, pp. 44-46, "It was on a day … Everybody knew it."

Guided Questions

1. What important event happens in the barn?
2. What does Templeton do when he hears the news?
3. How do the geese respond to Templeton's request?

Outline

I. ______________________________

II. ______________________________

III. ______________________________

Student Summary

In three sentences, summarize the passage. Say the sentences out loud to yourself. Then write them below.

____

____

____

____

____

____

____

____

____

____

Dictation

____

____

____

Reading Passage

Read *Charlotte's Web*, pp. 71-73, "I'm going to visit … a narrow escape."

Guided Questions

1. What does Avery see in the barn, and what does he want?
2. What happens to Avery?
3. Why doesn't he get the spider?

Outline

I. ______________________________

II. ______________________________

III. ______________________________

Student Summary

In three sentences, summarize the passage. Say the sentences out loud to yourself. Then write them below.

Dictation

Reading Passage

Read *Charlotte's Web*, pp. 99-101, "I'll tell you what … go the limit."

Guided Questions

1. What does Templeton do for Charlotte?
2. How does Charlotte test the accuracy of the new word?
3. What does she finally decide to do?

Outline

I. ______________________________

II. ______________________________

III. ______________________________

Student Summary

In three sentences, summarize the passage. Say the sentences out loud to yourself. Then write them below.

____

____

____

____

____

____

____

____

____

____

Dictation

____

____

____

Reading Passage

Read *Charlotte's Web*, pp. 114-115, "Wilbur was now … let him live."

Guided Questions

1. What happens to Wilbur as a result of the words in the web?
2. Why does this cause the other animals to worry?
3. What is actually true about Wilbur?

Outline

I. ______________________________

II. ______________________________

III. ______________________________

Student Summary

In three sentences, summarize the passage. Say the sentences out loud to yourself. Then write them below.

____

____

____

____

____

____

____

____

____

____

Dictation

____

____

____

Reading Passage

Read *Charlotte's Web*, pp. 133-135, "While Wilbur was … it can be done."

Guided Questions

1. What does Charlotte see as they settle in at the fair?
2. What does Charlotte do next?
3. What is Charlotte's impression of Wilbur's competition?

Outline

I. ____

II. ____

III. ____

Student Summary

In three sentences, summarize the passage. Say the sentences out loud to yourself. Then write them below.

Dictation

Reading Passage

Read *Charlotte's Web*, pp. 147-149, "As Wilbur was studying … rid of him for a while."

Guided Questions

1. What does Templeton announce?
2. What does Charlotte do when she hears the news?
3. How does Wilbur react?

Outline

I. ______________________________

II. ______________________________

III. ______________________________

Student Summary

In three sentences, summarize the passage. Say the sentences out loud to yourself. Then write them below.

____

____

____

____

____

____

____

____

____

____

Dictation

____

____

____

Reading Passage

Read *Charlotte's Web*, pp. 178-181, "Then came a quiet … and we like you."

Guided Questions

1. What unexpected event happens one spring morning?
2. How does this make Wilbur feel?
3. What occurs the next morning that surprises Wilbur?

Outline

I. ____________________

II. ____________________

III. ____________________

Student Summary

In three sentences, summarize the passage. Say the sentences out loud to yourself. Then write them below.

____

____

____

____

____

____

____

____

____

____

Dictation

____

____

____

Reading Passage

Read *A Bear Called Paddington*, pp. 20-22, "When they came out of the buffet … the driver slammed the window shut again."

Guided Questions

1. Why does the driver not want to give Paddington Bear a ride?
2. What does Paddington observe on his ride to the Browns?
3. How do the taxi driver's fears about Paddington come true?

Outline

I. ____________________

II. ____________________

III. ____________________

Student Summary

In three sentences, summarize the passage. Say the sentences out loud to yourself. Then write them below.

Dictation

Reading Passage

Read *A Bear Called Paddington*, pp. 35-39, "Oh, he's all right … I could have sworn I felt a spot of water."

Guided Questions

1. When does Paddington realize the tub is full?
2. What does Paddington draw on the bathroom floor with Mr. Brown's shaving cream?
3. How does Paddington try to bail out the water when the bathtub overflows?

Outline

I. ______________________________

II. ______________________________

III. ______________________________

Student Summary

In three sentences, summarize the passage. Say the sentences out loud to yourself. Then write them below.

____

____

____

____

____

____

____

____

____

____

Dictation

____

____

____

Reading Passage

Read *A Bear Called Paddington*, pp. 56-60, "Paddington decided the Underground … in the distance a bell began to ring."

Guided Questions

1. What happens when Paddington is separated from Mrs. Brown and Judy?
2. What happens to Paddington as he tries to run up the "down" escalator?
3. Why does Paddington push the emergency button?

Outline

I. ______________________________

II. ______________________________

III. ______________________________

Student Summary

In three sentences, summarize the passage. Say the sentences out loud to yourself. Then write them below.

____

____

____

____

____

____

____

____

____

Dictation

____

____

____

Reading Passage

Read *A Bear Called Paddington*, pp. 75-79, "Paddington kept his eyes closed … a door leading to one of the shop windows."

Guided Questions

1. Why can't Paddington see anything?
2. What happens when Paddington gropes around the room to try to locate the outside door of the shop?
3. Where does Paddington find himself and what does he accidentally do?

Outline

I. ____________________

II. ____________________

III. ____________________

Student Summary

In three sentences, summarize the passage. Say the sentences out loud to yourself. Then write them below.

____

____

____

____

____

____

____

____

____

Dictation

____

____

____

Reading Passage

Read *A Bear Called Paddington*, pp. 102-105, "The Browns occupied … when you particularly wanted to."

Guided Questions

1. Why does Mr. Brown not believe the painting to be his?
2. Why does Paddington think that he is in trouble again?
3. Who wins first prize at the exhibition?

Outline

I. ______________________________

II. ______________________________

III. ______________________________

Student Summary

In three sentences, summarize the passage. Say the sentences out loud to yourself. Then write them below.

Dictation

Reading Passage

Read *A Bear Called Paddington*, pp. 119-122, "Go away! … It shows what a great actor you are!"

Guided Questions

1. Why did Paddington go to see Sir Sealy Bloom during the play's intermission?
2. How had Paddington misinterpreted the play?
3. How does the actress, Sarah, console Sir Sealy Bloom?

Outline

I. ______________________________

II. ______________________________

III. ______________________________

Student Summary

In three sentences, summarize the passage. Say the sentences out loud to yourself. Then write them below.

____

____

____

____

____

____

____

____

____

Dictation

____

____

____

____

Reading Passage

Read *A Bear Called Paddington*, pp. 137-141, "Ten pounds! ... he soon went fast asleep."

Guided Questions

1. Why is Paddington disappointed when Judy wakes him up?
2. What does Mrs. Brown warn Jonathan, Judy, and Paddington about?
3. What happens to Paddington after he finishes building his sandcastle?

Outline

I. ______________________________

II. ______________________________

III. ______________________________

Student Summary

In three sentences, summarize the passage. Say the sentences out loud to yourself. Then write them below.

____

____

____

____

____

____

____

____

____

Dictation

____

____

____

____

Reading Passage

Read *A Bear Called Paddington*, pp. 162-164, "For my next trick … to one of your birthday parties."

Guided Questions

1. Who offers his watch for Paddington's magic trick?
2. Why does Paddington say the trick did not work?
3. How does Mr. Curry respond to his watch being shattered?

Outline

I. ______________________________

II. ______________________________

III. ______________________________

Student Summary

In three sentences, summarize the passage. Say the sentences out loud to yourself. Then write them below.

Dictation

Reading Passage

Read *Mr. Popper's Penguins*, pp. 2-4, "No one knew … he was reading about."

Guided Questions

1. What was Mr. Popper's occupation?
2. Why was Mr. Popper so absent-minded?
3. What did Mr. Popper regret most of all?

Outline

I. Mr. Popper was a house painter.
II. Mr. Popper was always dreaming of far away countries.
III. Mr. Popper regretted that he never visited the Poles.

Student Summary

In three sentences, summarize the passage. Say the sentences out loud to yourself. Then write them below.

Dictation

Reading Passage

Read *Mr. Popper's Penguins*, pp. 15-18, "You can imagine … those explorers at the Pole."

Guided Questions

1. What did Mr. Popper hear when he opened the package sent by Admiral Drake?
2. Describe the penguin.
3. How does the penguin behave in his new surroundings?

Outline

I. ______________________________

II. ______________________________

III. ______________________________

Student Summary

In three sentences, summarize the passage. Say the sentences out loud to yourself. Then write them below.

____

____

____

____

____

____

____

____

____

____

Dictation

____

____

____

Reading Passage

Read *Mr. Popper's Penguins*, pp. 49-50, "Mr. Popper soon found … comments on the new scene."

Guided Questions

1. Why was it not easy at first for Mr. Popper to take Captain Cook for a walk?
2. How did Captain Cook get down the stairs?
3. How do the neighbors react when they see Mr. Popper and Captain Cook out for a walk?

Outline

I. ______________________________

II. ______________________________

III. ______________________________

Student Summary

In three sentences, summarize the passage. Say the sentences out loud to yourself. Then write them below.

____

____

____

____

____

____

____

____

____

____

Dictation

____

____

____

Reading Passage

Read *Mr. Popper's Penguins*, pp. 64-65, "Captain Cook was not happy … to one hundred and five."

Guided Questions

1. What are some of the changes the Poppers observe in Captain Cook?
2. How do the Poppers eventually realize that something is wrong with Captain Cook?
3. What does the veterinary doctor think about Captain Cook's case?

Outline

I. ______________________________

II. ______________________________

III. ______________________________

Student Summary

In three sentences, summarize the passage. Say the sentences out loud to yourself. Then write them below.

____

____

____

____

____

____

____

____

____

____

Dictation

____

____

____

Reading Passage

Read *Mr. Popper's Penguins*, pp. 72-73, "Then I will … across the slippery ice."

Guided Questions

1. How does Mr. Popper temporarily help the penguins to live in a suitable climate?
2. How does this affect the Poppers?
3. How do the penguins feel about the change?

Outline

I. ______________________________

II. ______________________________

III. ______________________________

Student Summary

In three sentences, summarize the passage. Say the sentences out loud to yourself. Then write them below.

____

____

____

____

____

____

____

____

____

____

Dictation

____

____

____

Reading Passage

Read *Mr. Popper's Penguins*, pp. 104-105, "Mr. Greenbaum was the first … a lesson to them."

Guided Questions

1. What does Mr. Greenbaum think about the penguin act?
2. What are the terms of the contract he makes with Mr. Popper?
3. How do the Poppers feel about the contract?

Outline

I. ______________________________

II. ______________________________

III. ______________________________

Student Summary

In three sentences, summarize the passage. Say the sentences out loud to yourself. Then write them below.

____

____

____

____

____

____

____

____

____

____

Dictation

____

____

____

Reading Passage

Read *Mr. Popper's Penguins*, pp. 117-119, "The birds loved ... on canned shrimps."

Guided Questions

1. What did the penguins love about their new life?
2. How did the penguins behave when at a hotel?
3. Why was traveling so expensive for the Poppers?

Outline

I. ______________________________

II. ______________________________

III. ______________________________

Student Summary

In three sentences, summarize the passage. Say the sentences out loud to yourself. Then write them below.

Dictation

Reading Passage

Read *Mr. Popper's Penguins*, pp. 146-148, "Mr. Popper had gone down below … toward the sea."

Guided Questions

1. How does Mr. Popper feel as he says good-bye to the penguins?
2. What is the surprising turn of events?
3. Why does Admiral Drake want Mr. Popper to go on the expedition?

Outline

I. ______________________________

II. ______________________________

III. ______________________________

Student Summary

In three sentences, summarize the passage. Say the sentences out loud to yourself. Then write them below.

____

____

____

____

____

____

____

____

____

Dictation

____

____

____

____

Appendix

Supplemental Composition Lessons

Composition Lessons for *The Moffats*

Supplemental Lesson 1: Writing Sentences Smoothly

I. You have already learned that a sentence is a group of words expressing a complete thought. In order to write a good sentence, you must include a capital letter, a subject and a verb, and the appropriate end mark. Always ask yourself the following questions after writing a sentence:

- Did I express a complete thought?
- Did I include a subject and a verb?
- Did I include a capital letter and the appropriate end mark?

II. There is another question you also want to be asking about your sentences as you write them:

- Do my sentences read smoothly or are my ideas disjointed?

III. When you write sentences, it is important to join your ideas in such a way that they read smoothly. For example, the following sentences are disjointed:

The girl played with the puppy. The girl was small. The puppy was black and white.
Can you think of how to write the above sentences in one smooth sentence?
The small girl played with the black-and-white puppy.

Practice Exercise

Rewrite the following ideas in one clear sentence. (The practice sentences are all based on a literature selection. Try to imagine if the authors of your favorite books wrote in such a choppy way! Do you think you would enjoy reading their stories? Write the way your favorite authors do—clearly and smoothly.)

1. The room was mostly empty. Except there was one wardrobe. The wardrobe was big.

____

____

2. Lucy saw a strange person. He was carrying an umbrella. He was carrying several brown-paper parcels.

____

____

3. Mrs. Macready was not fond of children. She was the housekeeper.

____

____

4. On the sledge sat a lady. The lady was very tall. Her face was stern. Her face was pale.

____

____

5. At last the box of Turkish Delight was gone. Edmund had finished it. The Turkish delight was sweet.

____

____

Supplemental Lesson 2: Writing Sentences With Variety

I. As you know, a sentence must always have a subject and a verb. However, you do not want to begin every sentence with a subject followed by a verb. Your sentences will be dull and boring if you do so. Adverbs, clauses, and phrases can be used at the beginning of sentences to provide variety.

II. Read the following sentences:

1. Mary dusted the porcelain figurine carefully.
2. John cleans his room after he finishes his homework.
3. Jack and Andrew had a pillow fight at the sleepover.

III. Can you think of how to write these sentences with more variety?

1. Carefully, Mary dusted the porcelain figurine.
2. After he finishes his homework, John cleans his room.
3. At the sleepover, Jack and Andrew had a pillow fight.

Practice Exercise

Rewrite the following ideas in one clear sentence.

1. They felt coats around them, suddenly, instead of branches.

____

____

2. The queen kept on asking Edmund questions while he was eating Turkish Delight.

____

____

3. The children felt warmer when they had put on the coats from the wardrobe.

____

____

4. They set off walking briskly through the forest.

____

____

5. Peter, Susan, Edmund, and Lucy realized with shocked surprise that the beaver was talking to them.

____

____

* ***Note: Be careful not to revise every sentence this way. If you begin every sentence with an adverb, clause, or phrase, you will be just as monotonous. This exercise was simply to help you learn how to vary your sentences.***

Supplemental Lesson 3: Writing a Topic Sentence

A paragraph consists of several sentences developing one main idea or topic. Usually the first sentence of the paragraph tells what the paragraph is about and is known as the topic sentence. When you are writing a topic sentence, you should try to state the main idea of the whole paragraph in that one sentence. The other sentences in the paragraph will support the topic sentence.

Practice Exercise 1

Read the following paragraph and underline the topic sentence:

Mosquitoes are interesting insects to learn about. During the evening, mosquitoes are the most active. The female mosquitoes are the ones who bite, diluting human blood with their own saliva. It is the saliva that causes the bite to itch.

Practice Exercise 2

Choose two of the following topics and write a topic sentence for each of them. Indent these sentences because they will be the first sentence of a paragraph. Think through how you would plan out a paragraph based on your topic sentences. Remember that the topic sentence states the main idea of the whole paragraph.

a trip to the beach	playing basketball	my pet(s)
riding on a roller coaster	my best friend	my favorite subject
losing a classroom game	my favorite ice cream flavor	

1. ______________________________

____

____

2. ______________________________

____

____

* ***Note: Using the questions from the first lesson, don't forget to proof your topic sentences after you write them. Also, always make sure capitalization, punctuation, and spelling are perfect.***

Supplemental Lesson 4: Writing Supporting Sentences

The topic sentence of a paragraph is a general sentence. Additional information is needed to support the topic sentence. You will want to use either details, examples, or reasons to support the main idea of your paragraph.

Practice Exercise 1

Read the following paragraph. Underline the topic sentence and place a small star at the beginning of each supporting sentence.

My favorite book to read is *The Lion, the Witch and the Wardrobe*. Using memorable characters, such as the great lion Aslan, C. S. Lewis crafts a beautiful fantasy story. The setting of this story, Narnia, is an enchanted land full of adventure and magic. No matter how many times I reread *The Lion, the Witch and the Wardrobe*, I continue to be fascinated by the riveting plot.

Practice Exercise 2

In the space provided below, copy one of your topic sentences from Lesson 3. Develop at least three supporting sentences using details, examples, or reasons. Make sure you indent the first sentence of your paragraph. Be clear and interesting! Edit thoroughly!

Supplemental Lesson 5: Writing Sentences in the Correct Order

When you write supporting sentences for your paragraph, it is important to arrange them according to a specific plan. Your sentences should have a certain order, such as chronological or order of importance. Even if your individual sentences are well written but do not flow logically, your paragraph will not make sense.

Practice Exercise 1

Read the following paragraph and arrange the sentences in the correct order:

Through a magical wardrobe, they found themselves transported to a land called Narnia. After many strange and marvelous adventures, the children rescued Narnia and ruled instead of the witch for many years. Four children were sent to live in the country in an old house. Narnia, however, had been placed under a dreadful spell by an evil witch.

1. ______________________________

____

2. ______________________________

____

3. ______________________________

____

4. ______________________________

____

Practice Exercise 2

Check your paragraph from Practice Exercise 2 in Lesson 4 and make sure all of your sentences are arranged correctly.

Practice Exercise 3

Select another topic from the topics in Lesson 3. In the space provided below, indent and write a topic sentence stating the main idea of the whole paragraph. Then write at least three supporting sentences using details, examples, or reasons. Check to make sure your sentences are arranged correctly. Edit thoroughly!

____

____

____

____

____

____

Supplemental Lesson 6: Writing a Friendly Letter

Writing a friendly letter is a good way to keep in touch with family and friends who live far away. Study the example of a friendly letter below as you read through these instructions. When you write a friendly letter, you should include the following five parts:

1. **The heading** – your address and the date you wrote the letter
2. **The greeting** – the word "Dear" and the name of the person to whom you are writing
3. **The body** – the message you want to send
4. **The closing** – a way of saying goodbye, such as "Sincerely" or "With love"
5. **The signature** – your name

I. These five parts are positioned on your letter in the following ways:

1. **The heading** – in the upper right corner of the paper
2. **The greeting** – underneath the heading in the left margin
3. **The body** – underneath the greeting and kept in line with it, except where the first lines of paragraphs are indented
4. **The closing** – underneath the body, closer to the right margin
5. **The signature** – immediately after the closing and in line with it

II. Now that you know the parts of a friendly letter and where to position them, here are some guidelines about capitalization and punctuation:

- Capitalize all the words in the heading and the greeting, the first word of the closing, and the signature.
- Place commas between the route and the box number if there is one, between the city and the state, between the date and the year, after the greeting, and after the closing.

144 Kingman St.
Louisville, KY 40206
June 27, 2014

Dear Aunt Emily,

Hello! Greetings from Louisville, KY. I am getting very excited about my upcoming trip to Massachusetts to visit you and the rest of your family.

While we are up there, I hope we can take a few trips to the beach. I love many things about our new home in Louisville, but besides missing you and the family, I really miss living close to the ocean. It will be so much fun to soak up the sun and catch the waves together.

We have been very busy here this summer. The weather has been nice and warm, so we have been working a lot on our property, clearing overgrowth, weeding, mulching, and planting shrubs. It has been hard work, but very rewarding. How is your summer going? Are the kids out of school yet?

I am looking forward to seeing them and you very soon!

With love,
Drew

Practice Exercise

Practice writing a friendly letter on a sheet of notebook paper. Make sure to not only follow the guidelines to a friendly letter, but also make your letter interesting and enjoyable to read.

Supplemental Lesson 7: Addressing an Envelope

After you have written your friendly letter, you will need to mail it. In order to ensure that your letter reaches its intended destination, you will need to address an envelope properly. Study the example below while you read the instructions about addressing an envelope.

1. Your name and your address, called the return address, is placed in the upper left corner of the envelope. Always include this address in case the post office needs to return your letter.
2. The address of the person to whom you are writing is placed slightly below the middle and to the left of the center of the envelope. Include a title before the name of the person to whom you are addressing the letter.
3. Follow standard capitalization and punctuation rules while writing these addresses out.
4. Don't forget to apply the proper postage to the upper right corner of the envelope before mailing.

Drew Watson
144 Kingman St.
Louisville, KY 40206

STAMP

Mrs. Emily Wilkes
103 Country Lane
Bridgewater, MA 02304

Practice Exercise

Practice addressing an envelope properly. For fun, use the address of one of your classmates as well as your own for the return address.

____
____
____

STAMP

____
____
____

Supplemental Lesson 8: Writing a Book Report I

I. The First Paragraph:

Throughout your schooling, you will be required to write a variety of book reports. The next three lessons will be focused on a written book report. A written book report includes the following three paragraphs:

- information about the book
- a summary of the book
- an opinion about the book

II. In this lesson you will learn how to write the first paragraph. In the first paragraph you will want to give some general information about the book you read. This information should include the title of the book, the author, the year the book was published, and the genre (fantasy, biography, etc). You will also want to include 1-3 brief sentences summarizing the book. Study the example below before writing some practice paragraphs:

The Lion, the Witch and the Wardrobe is a fantasy novel, published in 1950 and written by C. S. Lewis. In this novel, four children are transported to the land of Narnia through a magical wardrobe. With the help of the great lion Aslan, the children must overturn the rule of an evil witch.

Practice Exercise

Select a book from off your classroom's library shelf that you have already read, and practice writing the first paragraph of a written book report in the space provided below. Don't forget to indent the first line. Be sure to underline the title of the book. Check all other punctuation, capitalization, and spelling also.

Supplemental Lesson 9: Writing a Book Report II

I. The Second Paragraph:

In the second paragraph of a written book report, you highlight what the book is about. If the book is a work of fiction, then you include information about the main characters, setting, and plot. If the book is a work of nonfiction, then you summarize the important information given. If the book is a biography, then you indicate the chief events and importance of that person's life. Although this paragraph is slightly longer than the first, 5-8 sentences, be careful not to get caught up in too many details. You are simply giving a general overview of the book.

II. Read the sample below and then complete the Practice Exercise:

During the Second World War, four siblings, named Peter, Susan, Edmund, and Lucy Pevensie, are sent to a big house in the country to escape the bombings in London. The magical wardrobe that transports them into Narnia is discovered first by Lucy during a game of hide-and-seek. Although Narnia is beautiful and magical, the children, except Edmund, are horrified to learn that it is ruled by a wicked witch who has made it always winter, but never Christmas. Sadly, Edmund betrays his family at first and enters the witch's service. The witch demands that Edmund die for his treason, but Aslan, the great lion who is the real ruler of Narnia, returns and gives up his life in Edmund's stead. However, since death cannot defeat one who has died in a traitor's place, Aslan is victorious over the witch and Narnia is restored. The Pevensie children are crowned as kings and queens of Narnia.

Practice Exercise

Using the same book you selected for the Practice Exercise in Lesson 8, write a second paragraph for a written book report in the space provided below. Remember, it should be 5-8 sentences. Indent the first line, as always, and check for punctuation, capitalization, and spelling mistakes.

Supplemental Lesson 10: Writing a Book Report III

I. The Third Paragraph:

In the third paragraph of a written book report, you state your opinion. In this opinion paragraph, you explain why you liked or disliked the book you are reporting on. Whatever your opinion is, you should give specific reasons and examples to support it. This paragraph should be 3-5 sentences and is the final paragraph of your book report.

II. Read the sample below and complete the Practice Exercise:

I thoroughly enjoyed reading *The Lion, the Witch and the Wardrobe* because C. S. Lewis did a remarkable job of drawing me into the story. The land of Narnia, with talking animals and magical creatures, was absolutely enchanting. The storyline was simple, yet rich with spiritual meaning. Aslan's sacrificial love reminded me of Christ's. For anyone seeking to read a good fantasy novel with overt redemptive themes, I would highly recommend *The Lion, the Witch and the Wardrobe*.

Practice Exercise 1

Using the same book you have practiced with from Lessons 8 and 9, complete your written book report with a 3-5 sentence opinion paragraph in the space provided below. Don't forget to indent and edit!

____

____

____

____

____

____

____

____

____

____

____

____

____

Practice Exercise 2

On a separate sheet of notebook paper, copy out all three paragraphs from Lessons 8, 9, and 10 of your written book report.

Reading Passage

Read *The Moffats*, pp. 8-11, "Jane recognized the newcomer. … see him right away."

Guided Questions

1. Who comes to the yellow house?
2. What does the man do, and how does Jane feel about it?
3. How does the rest of the family react to this event?

Outline

I. ____

II. ____

III. ____

Student Summary

In three sentences, summarize the passage. Say the sentences out loud to yourself. Then write them below.

Dictation

Reading Passage

Read *The Moffats*, pp. 47-50, "This time Rufus ... watching the schoolhouse disappear."

Guided Questions

1. Where does Rufus go?
2. What does he do in the freight car?
3. What happens to the boys that they don't expect?

Outline

I. ____

II. ____

III. ____

Student Summary

In three sentences, summarize the passage. Say the sentences out loud to yourself. Then write them below.

Dictation

Reading Passage

Read *The Moffats*, pp. 98-102, "Again they left the warm safety … laughing all at once."

Guided Questions

1. Why does Peter Frost come to the Moffats' house?
2. How is he convinced of the ghost?
3. What does he do as a result?

Outline

I. ______________________________

II. ______________________________

III. ______________________________

Student Summary

In three sentences, summarize the passage. Say the sentences out loud to yourself. Then write them below.

____

____

____

____

____

____

____

____

____

____

Dictation

____

____

____

Reading Passage

Read *The Moffats*, pp. 116-119, "Then Miss Chichester said … applause rocked the hall."

Guided Questions

1. What must Joe do that he is unprepared for?
2. What happens during the performance?
3. How do Joe and the audience respond?

Outline

I. ______________________________

II. ______________________________

III. ______________________________

Student Summary

In three sentences, summarize the passage. Say the sentences out loud to yourself. Then write them below.

Dictation

Reading Passage

Read *The Moffats*, pp. 125-128, "The car stopped in front … on her lashes again."

Guided Questions

1. Who comes to visit the Moffat family?
2. What does he say about Rufus, and what does he do as he leaves?
3. How is the family comforted after hearing this news?

Outline

I. ______________________________

II. ______________________________

III. ______________________________

Student Summary

In three sentences, summarize the passage. Say the sentences out loud to yourself. Then write them below.

____

____

____

____

____

____

____

____

____

____

Dictation

____

____

____

Reading Passage

Read *The Moffats*, pp. 161-163, "It was lucky there were four ... of that she was sure."

Guided Questions

1. What is the Moffat family rule?
2. What does Jane do with the five cents she is given?
3. How does she feel as she eats her treat?

Outline

I. ______________________________

II. ______________________________

III. ______________________________

Student Summary

In three sentences, summarize the passage. Say the sentences out loud to yourself. Then write them below.

____

____

____

____

____

____

____

____

____

____

Dictation

____

____

____

Reading Passage

Read *The Moffats*, pp. 181-184, "'No,' shouted Jane … leave us alone for awhile.'"

Guided Questions

1. What does Jane decide she must do?
2. How does she carry out her decision?
3. What is the result of Jane's plan?

Outline

I. ______________________________

II. ______________________________

III. ______________________________

Student Summary

In three sentences, summarize the passage. Say the sentences out loud to yourself. Then write them below.

____

____

____

____

____

____

____

____

____

____

Dictation

____

____

____

Reading Passage

Read *The Moffats*, pp. 204-208, "Slowly she went out … to the yellow house like lightning."

Guided Questions

1. How is Jane feeling as she visits the Moffats' new house?
2. What happens to change Jane's outlook?
3. What does she think about moving now?

Outline

I. ______________________________

II. ______________________________

III. ______________________________

Student Summary

In three sentences, summarize the passage. Say the sentences out loud to yourself. Then write them below.

Dictation